Si~ Starks,
ank
you
~~iu your years
of care. Many
are better
because
of YOU!
Love you so,
Tisa
Holley

WHO CARES!

Answering Difficult Questions
Asked by Today's Educators

Tisa M. Holley

Foreword by Sandra Holley

Copyright © 2018 Tisa M. Holley

All rights reserved. No part of this publication may be reproduced, distributed, or transmitted in any form or by any means, including photocopying, recording, or other electronic or mechanical methods, without the prior written permission of the publisher, except in the case of brief quotations, embodied in reviews and certain other non-commercial uses permitted by copyright law.

ISBN-13: 978-0-692-08377-2

DEDICATION

This book is dedicated to my Godchildren—
Alana, Aidan, Braden, Carter, and Kennedy—
and their friends, the future educators, coaches,
mentors, and leaders of our world.

TABLE OF CONTENTS

ACKNOWLEDGEMENTS

A special Thank You to . . .

My Lord and Savior, Jesus Christ for His example as a servant leader and demonstrating compassion to others.

. . . I just want to follow in Your footsteps.

My Mom and Dad for loving me and teaching me that "I can do all things through Christ which strengthens me" and encouraging me in ALL my endeavors.

. . . I just want to make you proud.

Current and former superintendents, headmasters, principals, supervisors, and colleagues for developing me as an educator.

. . . I just want to reciprocate your aid with future educators.

Current and former parents for entrusting me with your most prized possession—your CHILDREN!

. . . I just want to help.

Tim Young for introducing me to Self-Publishing School. The Launch Team—Tiara, Bud, B. Young, Marita, Shannon, and Mouse—for making this dream a reality.

. . . I just want to make a greater impact.

Antoinette "Toni" Foxx, my editor, for your patience with me.

. . . I just want it to be EXCELLENT.

My current and former students for pushing me to be my best!

. . . I just want you to soar!

I love you!

Foreword – How It Originated

"For I know the plans I have for you, declares the Lord, plans to prosper you and not to harm you, plans to give you hope and a future. Then you will call on me and come and pray to me and I will listen to you. You will seek me and find me when you seek me with all your heart."

Jeremiah 29:11-13 (NIV)

My plans were not to become a teacher or to work with children. I am one of eight children. Why would I want to work with children?

But God!

I just knew that I was to become a fashion designer. Why a fashion designer? Well, because God taught me how to sew. Every night, while I slept, He taught me how to sew (NO, I am not crazy). My family knew that I was crazy, but eventually, they believed me after my Mother bought me a sewing machine and I made ALL of my clothes.

I had prayed and asked God what was His plan for my life. In His answer, He blessed me with a little baby girl named Tisa. It was at that time when I looked at her and held her next to my heart that my heart changed, and I just started loving children.

God's plan for me on the earth was to become a teacher. I loved and cared for my students, and they knew it. I saw my students as individuals, not a group of students; and I treated them as my own. I was everything to my students! I helped pay rent and bought food and clothes for them. I visited their homes and held conferences at their dining room table with their parents while Tisa sat in their homes doing her homework. Some parents came to my home to have conferences because they knew that I had their child's BEST interest in my heart. At the same time, Tisa sat at her desk in our home and did her homework; but I knew that she was listening and observing her Mother talking to her parents.

Children must know and feel that you genuinely care for them. I was very consistent with my children. I greeted ALL of my students at the classroom door with a handshake and said, "Good Morning" EVERYDAY (180 days each year take away the days that I was not at school). That was my way of touching and agreeing that every student would have a GREAT day.

My children would share situations about their families with me. One of my student's father was a police officer and would tell my student that he would be over to his house to see him over the weekend. My student would come to school distraught because his dad did not come to see him. My student knew that I would take care of the situation. After a brief, intense call to his Dad saying, "Your son needs to see you, and I need you to come to the school to see your son." Momentarily, I would see the police car pull up in the parking lot of the school. I would find an empty room so that they could have some father–son time.

I would give my parents advice on how to raise and to discipline their children. I would repeat advice to my parents over and over and over again.

I even sat in a funeral home with one of my students and his sister when his mother passed away (only me and the two children). Imagine me, the two children, and the Mothers' body. My goodness that was an experience! I loved and cared for my students with my whole heart.

God instructed me to:

> "Do not be afraid of their faces, For I *am* with you to deliver you," says the Lord. Then the Lord put forth His hand and touched my mouth, and the Lord said to me: "Behold, I have put My words in your mouth. See, I have this day set you over the nations and over the kingdoms, to root out and to pull down, to destroy and to throw down, to build and to plant."
>
> Jeremiah 1:8-10 (NKJV)

I knew that whatever you do, work at it with all your Heart, as working for the Lord, not for human masters, since you know that you will receive an inheritance from the Lord as a reward. It is the Lord Christ you are serving. Colossians 3:23-24 (NIV)

I have more to tell, but this book is not about me—it is about Tisa's experience with her students. Genesis 1:11 says . . . these seeds will produce the kinds . . . from which they came. And that is what happened.

Tisa's story about Caring for her students now begins!!

Sandra J. Holley
Retired Educator, 35 years
Tisa's proud mom

Introduction

Who Cares? Why Care?

These are questions that students and teachers throughout the world ask themselves. Students are asking, "Who cares about me?" "Who feels interested in me?" "Who's devoted to me?" "I can't tell from my parents. I can't tell from the news. WHO CARES ABOUT ME?"

On the other hand, teachers/educators are asking, "Why care? Why help? Why become invested? Why become concerned about students that are ungrateful; students that come to class unprepared; parents that are always blaming me as the problem; or administrators that have expected deliverables that seem irrelevant to student success?"

This word "care" is important for the future success of children throughout this nation. Merriam-Webster's Dictionary defines "care" as

1. To feel interest in something

2. To be concerned about

3. to have a liking, fondness

4. To provide help, protection, or supervision to

5. To look after and provide for the needs of

6. To be devoted to; to think the world of

Synonyms for the word "care" are to be devoted to, to think the world of, to be fond of; while the antonyms of "care" are to disregard, to ignore, to overlook.

As you read this book, you will find the answers to Why Care? You will find the answers for Who Cares? Because there are men and women throughout history that have shown care, that have totally changed the trajectory of success for many little boys and little girls that are now productive citizens in our country.

Let's look at . . .

3rd grade – Sister Patti

"This young girl can be a dancer. Place her in a dance school and watch her grow." **That's care.**

Dr. Amenta Crouch –

Every day from 6th to 12th grade, she greeted every student in her building with a "Good morning!" On the other side of the "Good morning" was a connection. She would look each student in his or her eyes, inquiring about the night before and encouraging them about the day on the horizon. She showed up to sporting events, classrooms, and the cafeteria. Why? Because she cared. **Why?** Because she was fond of us.

Dr. Willette O. Wright –

Another school leader who greeted her students but did not leave you there. She provided encouraging words and periodic check ins. Not just in elementary, middle, or high school, but even in college and in life after college.

When you care, care never stops. Care never ends. Care continues. When one cares, it is reciprocated, causing care to become contagious. Contagious like a cough; contagious like a yawn. Care is care. Others notice it, desire it, become it, and passes it on.

Care is power.

For almost 20 years, I have had the opportunity to work with young people in grades K – 12th grade. Through these pages, not only will you see success stories, but also the answer to the question, "Why Care?" You will read the stories of my former students and the impact that their lives had on me and the need for their voices (and voices similar) to be heard.

These are not just regular stories. They are stories of impact. They are life-changing. They are stories that have never been told, and now is the time for their voices to be heard.

Unit 1 – What Is Care?

1. To feel interest in something

2. To be concerned about

3. To have a liking, fondness

4. To provide help, protection, or supervision to

5. To look after and provide for the needs of

6. To be devoted to; to think the world of

On average, school-age children spend 25–35 hours a week at school with teachers, staff, and school leaders. In a research study on how children and adolescents spend their time by Larson and Verma (1999), they noted that "the school day varies from 5-7 hours across the U.S. and European nations" (p. 712). With the increase of time spent at school, there will be a decrease in time spent at home with family. Larson and Verma (1999) adds that "in populations where children attend school, there is a decline in time spent with family and in the homestead area at the age of school entry" (p. 723).

With children spending less time with family, it becomes imperative that educators, coaches, mentors, school leaders, and even policymakers, understand and embrace their role as caregivers. Not only will they teach academics but will also provide many non-instructional lessons. They will aid in the character and social-emotional development of their students.

As the educators, we must begin with the basic tenets of caregiving.

1. Building rapport and establishing a relationship

2. Building self-efficacy in your students

3. Providing support

Over the next three lessons, you will examine these tenets, be introduced to students that portray the lesson taught, and reflect on your current practices. At the end of some lessons, you can also extend the lesson with an application exercise.

Let's get to it!

". . . Caring is selflessness and love for another person; and as distinctive as each individual is, the look of caring is as unique and, when devoutly given, is a priceless treasure."

Paige McLaughlin, class of 2009

Lesson 1 – Rapport & Relationship Building

"Getting to Know Me"

One of my mentors taught me that "rules without relationship equals rebellion." If your students know you and that you care about them, they will do WHATEVER you ask or instruct them to do.

Let's also examine another incorrectly used term, "respect." Like the chorus in Aretha Franklin's song, "R-E-S-P-E-C-T," young people will "sock it to" you if they don't know you. Merriam Webster's Dictionary defines respect as "esteem for a person; the condition of being esteemed or honored."

Students can neither respect nor disrespect people that they don't know. Disrespect happens when there has been a breach in the relationship and should not be overlooked. When the adult-child relationship is mended, it teaches the child that they can relate to adults and further strengthens the bond.

When getting to know children, I must believe

1. That we are created equally,

2. That I need them, and

3. That they are valuable.

In every encounter with a child, I must make eye contact. My non-verbal communication and body language must be non-threatening. Give a listening ear. These simple gestures, over time, open the door to their hearts. It screams, "I care."

This entire book highlights lessons taught by over 500 bright and valuable students. These lessons further demonstrate the fact that we need our children and that they are valuable.

Dustin's Story

In a senior Life Skills course, all students were asked to present one personal attribute that they embody. Some selected self-control; others chose joy. Dustin presented peace. As a young teacher, I thought, "how can this teen understand or embody PEACE. I don't even have PEACE!"

Dustin stood before the class with his board and began to define peace as "calm delight." As he spoke, he closed his eyes and shared how he could be peaceful despite what he saw around him. The class and I could not help but to close our eyes to attempt to experience peace with Dustin.

As the year continued, I watched Dustin. I never saw him discouraged, defeated, or disconnected from his peers. I admired his ability to remain peaceful. It was Dustin (yes, a student) that taught me that I could have peace. This must have been my first lesson taught by a student. . . the first of many!!!

Homework

1. Identify one student that taught you a lesson?

_____

_____

2. Why is this lesson significant?

_____

_____

_____

_____

_____

_____

_____

Extended Lesson – Would you tell a student when he or she has taught you a lesson? Explain your response.

_____

_____

_____

_____

_____

_____

_____

_____

_____

_____

As I approach 20 years of working with young people, I can't help but to reflect on my humble beginnings. At the age of 16, I was assigned to teach dance to elementary school children in grades 1 – 8.

This next lesson was taught because of not building a rapport with students that eventually had to be mended.

Priscilla's Story

To manage the size of the dance class, it was necessary to group the dancers. The groups were based on skill level, concentration, and cooperation. Dancers were categorized in three groups: "A" – principal dancers, "B" – alternates, or "C" – not allowed to dance. Often the "C" group was the "threat" to maintain the order. After auditions, students would receive their category.

As a 2nd grade student, Priscilla got a "C" decision. This affected Priscilla for years. Other opportunities were presented to her to dance or to participate in movement, but she would decline.

Several years later, Priscilla and I crossed paths again. This time I was a mature, certified teacher. Priscilla was having difficulty in learning from me. Eventually I suggested that she remain after class for tutoring. She and her parents agreed. As the session began, she started to cry. Quite puzzled, I asked, "What's wrong?"

She bellows, "You told me to 'C' you later, and I never got a chance to dance." Although that event took place approximately 10 years prior, it still affected her and was now hindering her academic progress.

It became evident that we needed that conversation. I apologized for how I made her feel and reassured her that I only wanted to extract the very best in her now as my student.

Reminders –

1. I must view my students as valuable; they can teach me a lesson!

2. Rules without relationship equals rebellion; I must get to know my students.

3. It's okay to apologize when you have done wrong by a student; this keeps the relationship healthy and says that you care.

Once a child knows that you care, you must tell him (or her) that he CAN!!!

Lesson 2 – Self–Efficacy

"You can . . ."

Self-efficacy, as defined by psychologist Albert Bandura, is "one's belief in one's ability to succeed in specific situations or to accomplish a task." It is also defined as "confidence in one's own ability to achieve intended results." Self-efficacy is steep in an individual's external experiences and their self-perception. The essence of self-efficacy is that "if you tell a person that he can, he will; if you tell a person that he can't, he won't."

In a research study of students with disabilities, Yssel et al. (2007) explained how parents in a focus group "desired to see her child living in a normalized society . . . she must learn. Parents also commented on their child's determination to be like everybody else. These children had to experience major adjustments and face many challenges but were determined to fit in" (p. 363). This persistence and commitment to motivating every child is paramount.

Sometimes one's self-efficacy is developed indirectly. I can recall one of the first projects that I completed in 5th grade—the "Eye" can. The teacher instructed us to bring in an emptied can, magazines, and glue. For the next few days, she instructed us to cut out as many eyes as we could, followed by gluing them on the can. When we were done, she told us that that can was to hold our pens and pencils when we were in class. Additionally, it was to remind us every day that we COULD do well in her class!

As the year progressed and the courses became difficult, I would reach for a writing utensil and be reminded that "I can!" The "eye" can followed me the next school year to keep me mindful and encouraged. This teacher and many like her really worked hard to build our confidence in our abilities. **This must continue in our schools.**

Teachers, staff, and school leaders must be reminded of their influence on the confidence in students. Some students are intrinsically motivated, but most are motivated externally. The words of an adult can "make or break" them.

This lesson is further solidified by Sadie, a student that had been retained and had not experienced much success in school.

Sadie's Story

When I met Sadie, she was not reading or writing on grade level. To make gains, a tutoring schedule was developed for her to have one-on-one sessions with me. Overtime, I noticed the growth. Her peers would also help her in pronouncing words.

During the 2nd quarter, it was common for me to conclude the poetry unit with a poetry explanation paper and recitation. After several weeks of preparation, it was presentation day. As was customary, I stood at my door to greet my students, "Good morning!"

On this morning, Sadie's eyes were red as a beet. "What's wrong, Sadie?" I asked. "I can't do the presentation!" she cries. "Yes, you can!" I commented. "No, I can't," she bellows. Reassuringly I looked Sadie in the eyes and asked her if she had prepared. She said, "Yes, but I can't seem to remember." Before I let her enter the classroom, I told her to do her best and that I would support her through the presentation by giving her lead-in words. By the end of the conversation, she had stopped crying and was able to enter the classroom.

Knowing that I, too, was concerned about Sadie, I selected her last to present to protect her dignity. Sadie stood before the class and with a quivering voice, she stated the title of her poem. As she began, she started to cry, but I was prepared to read the poem for her if she needed it.

Sadie, while crying, finished the first line of the poem. Then she finished the first stanza. Still crying, she recites the 2nd stanza. (By the way, she had to present at least 20 lines.) By the end of the third stanza, I find myself crying with Sadie. When Sadie finished reciting her poem, I stood up, and she ran into my arms. Her peers cheered.

Drying my tears, I said, "I told you that you could do it!" She adds, ". . . and I did it all by myself!!" You got it; I never had to say anything to get Sadie through her poem. I just had to tell her that she COULD do it!!!

For the next four years, Sadie became one of my favorite students. Although I was not her teacher, she would keep me informed of her curricular and extra-curricular activities. I became one of her cheerleaders. Regardless of the milestones in her life, she knew that she could count on me to instill confidence in her abilities by reminding her that she can!!

Homework

1. Who is the person(s) that continues to remind you that You can?

_____

_____

_____

2. What affect has this person had on the choices that you have made?

_____

_____

_____

Extended Lesson – Contact the person to express your sincerest gratitude for his or her contribution to your life. Share what you are doing now.

Reminders –

1. If you tell a person that he can, he will; if you tell a person that he can't, he won't.

2. Teachers, staff, and school leaders have an influence on the confidence in students. The words of an adult can "make or break" them.

Once a child knows that he or she can, it is beneficial to show your support.

"Care is evidenced by investment. That can be the investment of attention, time, energy, or resources. These investments are a tangible representation of concern put to action."

—Joshua Lowery, class of 2015

Lesson 3 – Support

"I KNOW that I can, but can you help me?"

As a young child, I was taught Philippians 4:13, a scripture that says that I can do all things through Christ which strengthens me. This scripture has guided me throughout my life, for rarely have I taken on a status of defeat. Although I enjoy victories, it is impossible to win without supporters.

There have been many people that have helped me in my pursuits—parents, family, teachers/professors, principals, supervisors, colleagues, friends, students, and even strangers. Support is necessary in accomplishing any task, big or small.

As educators, we must understand our role as supporters of our students. Some students will have the boldness to ask for help, while others will not have the courage to seek your assistance even though it is needed. This will require you to have a level of student awareness and a willingness to see a student in need and to offer support.

A similar tenet of confidence had been taught to Nike. His parents had instilled confidence in him, causing him to be quite determined. Read more to see how needful your support is for our future leaders.

Nike's Story

It was Nike's tenth grade year. He had not been too involved in extracurricular activities; however, he had this new idea. He wanted the school to offer a flag football team. As the athletic director, I shared this request with our principal. He said that there was no money for a new sports team at the time, but if the students organized themselves and raised funds for the team, he would allow it. I shared this information with Nike and told him that I was willing to support him.

Not sure of how Nike was going to take this information, he said, "Ok!" Within a week, Nike came by my office with two fundraiser ideas and a student team of three peers that were willing to work. I was impressed and excited! The principal approved the fundraisers, and they happened.

After raising the funds, I gave Nike and his staff sports equipment catalogs to identify and to select the items to be purchased. They made their decisions, and I ordered them. At the first game of the season, Nike's teammates congratulated him for his leadership and follow-through in making their inaugural season a success.

This was just the beginning for Nike and his business pursuits. Three years later, he entered college as a business major and graduated four years later with a bachelor's degree in business administration.

Homework

1. How can you support your students/athletes now in honing their gifts, talents, and abilities?

_____

_____

_____

_____

_____

_____

_____

_____

_____

_____

_____

_____

2. Are you willing to help? Explain your response.

_____

_____

_____

_____

_____

_____

_____

_____

_____

Reminders –

1. It is impossible to win without supporters; educators must be members of a student's support team!

2. Some students will have the boldness to ask for help, while others will not have the courage to seek your assistance even though it is needed.

Care is shown through relationship-building, confidence-building, and support given.

Unit 2 – What Does Care Look Like?

Let's begin this unit by reviewing our definitions of care.

1. To feel interest in something

2. To be concerned about

3. To have a liking, fondness

4. To provide help, protection, or supervision to

5. To look after and provide for the needs of

6. To be devoted to; to think the world of

Care is an action verb. Care follows the idea that it is better to "show me than to tell me." Often, the validity of a person's words is only confirmed through the actions.

There is another cliché that states "talk is cheap!" Most school-aged children would agree. They might even say that talk is cheap; however, your actions are priceless. Our actions, our follow-through, and our ability to refrain from being situationally impulsive is priceless.

Our actions have and will continue "to make or to break" the lives of our young people. If we say that we are going to do something, we must. So many of today's children and youth are already disappointed because they have been let down by so many people. As the educators, coaches, mentors, school leaders, and even policymakers, we must be something different. We must make sure school is the place where they are nurtured, loved, forgiven, supported, served, helped, taught, trained, and empowered, which by the way, are action verbs.

From their mouths . . .

Approximately 65 current and former students were asked, "What does care look like?" This is how they answered.

"It would seem easy to limit care to a smile, a hug, or any other act of pleasantry from one person to another on the basis of love; but care is this and more. Care is a faceless love that is willing to sacrifice feelings and break hearts. It comes in the form of a teacher who is willing to correct an unruly student. A coach who would bench a starter that has broken a team rule the day before a championship game. A parent whose discipline brings their child to tears. These are only a few facets of care, but they each look different."

—Justin Banks, class of 2015

"Care is having compassion even when there is no reward or recognition. Care is extending yourself to others to be of service to help make their day a little brighter or lives a little easier."

—Alisha Cooper, class of 2010

"Care is the nurturing of something for its greater good."

—Katrina McSwain, class of 2018

"Care looks like going the extra mile for others. Care is going out of the way to benefit the good of others. Care is showing someone how much you appreciate them by the actions and condition of your heart."

—Kalyn Banks, class of 2016

"Care looks like being there for one another in a supportive manner . . . helping them to succeed through life or simply just being someone who they can lean on in times of good and bad. To me, care can be mistaken for niceness, but I believe, care is something that is done from your heart."

—Naomi McSwain, class of 2013

"Care, to me, is genuine concern for a person's wellbeing, interests, and physical, mental, social, emotional, and financial development."

—Artaveya Ingram, class of 2010

"Care looks like giving things important in your life time and attention. It is deciding to put others before yourself at all costs. That looks like Sis. Tisa Holley telling a young man, whose childhood was filled with getting in trouble and having a bad reputation filed behind his name, that he would someday be on the Honor Society, do great things, and graduate from high school. All of which, at the time, seemed like such hopelessness in the form of words to a young boy. To his surprise but not Sis. Holley's, all of this did happen. Care is inputting yourself in one to make them better and pulling out of them what they may fail to realize is there. Caring is making a choice to care because caring is the right thing to do. It is a heart condition and something for those who want the best for themselves and others."

—Dennis Gray, Jr., class of 2016

Lesson 1 –
Something Familiar

"My Mom's Example"

The word "familiar" is defined as something "frequently seen or experienced; of everyday occurrence." Care is what I saw and experienced as I watched my mom. From her days in middle schools to an elementary school and back to middle schools, I saw a lady give of her time, her attention, and sometimes her finances for the betterment of her students.

There were many afternoons when I completed homework at the dinner table of another family because the only time that a parent was available was in the evening. During the meeting, my mom would not refrain from telling the truth. She spoke with such great passion and concern for the student. Although she was the teacher of real content, she placed even greater attention on the long-term outcomes of the child. She would address the student's choices, friend selection, and following the rules. Before the end of the meeting, the parent would be threatening the child, saying things like, "Ms. Holley had better not have to call me again or you are going to get it."

Rarely did we have to visit a home twice!

Care also resembled us purchasing groceries for the families of students that were in need. She would say things like, "Tee, we are about to stop pass _____ house, so I can drop off this food." She sometimes would even buy uniforms or outfits for special events if she knew a family could not afford it. The irony in all of this giving was that there were times that she would show me her checkbook, which reflected very little to take care of her and me for two weeks . . . but our needs were always met.

What I would consider to be the most significant example of care is when my mom became the honorary grandmother to one of her students when his mother passed. The family of the deceased knew the relationship that my mom had with the student and his sister, and they asked her to attend the family viewing with the children before the funeral. Supportively she agreed.

She took the two children by their hands and entered the room where their mom would be rolled. They patiently awaited her arrival. Once the funeral home staff left the room, there were only four people in the room—the deceased, her two children, and my mom. For almost two hours, they fellowshipped. The children sang songs; they talked to their mom; they hugged; they talked. When it was time to go, my mom reminded them that that would be their last time with their mom. They understood and simply placed their heads in my mom's lap. For another year or so, she remained in touch with them until she called one day, and the number was no longer in service. There are times that I wonder about those two students. How are they? What are they doing?

Although my path has not crossed with theirs, oftentimes, my mom (and I) will run into her former students; and both parties will get so excited. The former students will always start out by repeating something that she said to them when they were in her class. They will give her an update on their life and sometimes their parents.

Avery's Story

Throughout school, Avery had been an all-star. She was very smart, quite involved in extracurricular activities, and well-liked by her peers and teachers. I taught Avery in the 9th grade, and we really connected. She learned quickly and always requested more challenging work. She eventually became one of my afterschool tutors and volunteered afterschool through her senior year.

During the tutoring session, she would sound and look like me. She was patient in her delivery, she would get ultra-excited when her students answered the questions correctly, and she did not allow her students to quit. I loved watching her in action, and I would periodically tell her parents of the excellent job that she was doing.

One day, her dad pulled me to the side to share that her mom was sick. Apparently, I didn't understand to what extent she was ill. Within maybe two months, I received a phone call telling me that Avery's mom had passed.

I immediately called another colleague, and we went to be with the family. While visiting, Avery's dad pulled me to the side again. This time, he asked if I would be willing to help him in raising Avery. In that moment, I had a flashback to my mom and her "favorite family's time of bereavement." I was honored. I answered, "certainly."

Over the next few months, Avery and I went shopping for special events, went on trips, had really good conversations and meals together. She had opportunities to meet some of my friends and so much more. Avery even had her room at my house for those times that she needed to come over. Despite the situation, everything seemed so very perfect. Gradually, I lost contact with Avery. I would call for her and would not get a response.

Like my mom, I do wonder how Avery is. I loved Avery like she was birthed by me. I continue to pray weekly for Avery, desiring that she maximizes all of the gifts and talents, skills and abilities that were birthed inside of her; for she will always be an all-star in my mind.

Homework

1. Who are some of the "Avery's" in your life (children you cared about but lost connection with due to unforeseen circumstances)?

_____

_____

_____

_____

_____

2. What did you desire for your "Avery" and why?

_____

_____

_____

_____

_____

_____

Reminders –

1. Care is something familiar—something seen or experienced frequently.

2. Care, done correctly, will be repeated.

"Care looks like interest. Genuine interest in another being not physical but mentally and emotionally. The kind of interest that can look beyond the outer parts of someone. The interest that helps you look deep into a being and determine what makes them, THEM. The interest that helps you pull back the layers of others and break down the walls that they have built to keep others out. 'Let each of you look not only to his own interests, but also to the interests of others' Philippians 2:4."

—Keishara Foxx, class of 2010

Lesson 2 –
Something Familial

"Can We Be Family?"

Not only is care something familiar, but also it is something familial. Familial is defined as "characteristic of family." There is a popular quotation that says, "Home is where the heart is." For many students through the years, school has become home because of the hearts, care, and attention given by teachers, coaches, and other staff.

Students will often confide in a staff member as they would a mom or a dad, a sister or a brother, an aunt or an uncle. Sometimes they will invite you to their special events or tell you when their birthday is with hopes that you would celebrate them like family would.

As the educator, you need to ask yourself some questions–

1. How often do I actually listen to my students?

2. Am I willing to give my personal time for a student?

3. Do I view my students with their present situation in mind or with the future possibilities and success in mind?

You see, family is built on the quality of time together, the ability to listen without judgement, and the desire to promote success—to see and to express your BEST!

Every student may not become your family, but the environment that you are creating should resemble something familial and desirable.

Keyona's Story

As with many first-year educators, I knew that I wanted to make a difference in the life of children but was not sure as to how it would happen.

I met Keyona during my first year of teaching. I was 22 years old and the middle school physical education teacher, and Keyona was 11 years old. She had a pretty outgoing personality and was quite athletic. In addition to being her teacher, I was also one of her basketball coaches. Periodically, Keyona would stop by my office on her way to practice "just to chat." The next time she brought her best friend, Evelyn, with her, and we would just chat. These visits started to happen on a regular basis, and the chats became more like conversations about EVERYTHING.

They continued through 7th and 8th grade. Eventually I purchased afternoon snacks for the girls to eat when they came by and would even be concerned on days when they did not stop by. They would definitely share what caused them not to visit.

It was during Keyona's 8th grade year that I learned that she saw me as more than her teacher and her coach. During one of the visits, she says, "Coach Holley! Can you be my Godmom? I have a Godmom, but I don't really know her." I was shocked that this child wanted me to a part of her family. I agreed.

In the process, my name changed from Coach Holley to Momma T; and with permission from her parents, we spent more time together. At the end of her 8th grade year, I moved back home to Maryland. I was quite hesitant to move because of our relationship. I was not sure of how she should would take it or if our relationship would continue. That concern was not a problem.

Keyona and Evelyn would call me throughout high school and send silly pictures to keep me in the loop. They spent one Christmas in Maryland with me and my family. I attended their high school graduation, supported Keyona throughout college, celebrated her college graduation, and other milestones.

Today when asked if I have any children, I answer, "No, but I have four godchildren." Knowing that Keyona was my first godchild. I am so very proud of my godchild because she has become everything that we chatted about when she was a child—a college grad, a dedicated wife, a loving mom, a loyal friend, and a hard-working young woman.

Homework

1. When a student sees you as more than an educator, how do you handle the relationship?

_____

_____

_____

_____

_____

_____

_____

_____

_____

_____

_____

_____

_____

_____

2. Why is compassionate listening important?

_____

_____

_____

_____

_____

_____

_____

_____

Extended Lesson – Write a letter to that familial student sharing what you see and desire long-term for him or her.

Reminders –

1. Care is familial—characteristic of family.

2. Every student may not become your family, but the environment that you are creating should resemble something familial and desirable.

"Someone who takes the time to get to know you—understand how you think, considers your feelings and is willing to go the extra mile to make sure you succeed."

Brandyn White, class of 2013

Lesson 3 – Something Like Follow-through

"... But that was what you said?"

Care is familiar, care is familial, but care is also follow-through. Follow-through is if I say that I am going to do something I will do it. In a previous chapter, we mentioned that "talk is cheap." Everybody has something to say, but only those who care will follow through with it.

It is in follow through that trust is built or trust is destroyed. A lack of follow though is viewed by students as empty promises. As educators, coaches, mentors, and school leaders, we must be mindful of the "promises" that we make to our students. We must be aware of overcommitting because our students are counting on us to do what we say.

When you care, you will follow through regardless of the personal sacrifice of time, effort, or resources.

Melvin's Story

It was the summer prior to Melvin's senior year. He and his mom had scheduled an appointment to review his class schedule and to discuss some additional options. When they arrived, his mom mentioned that Melvin had not been feeling well and that they had just left the doctor's office.

As the meeting continued, I encountered a roadblock that was going to prevent me from being able to finish his schedule in the meeting. I needed to discuss a matter with my principal and get back to the family on Monday. I informed them that I would call on Monday afternoon. They were okay with this decision.

Over the weekend, Melvin had to be admitted to the hospital and was told that he needed a transplant. This information was shared with me on Monday afternoon when I called Melvin's mom back with our decision.

As his mom was sharing, I interjected, "Have you told anyone at the school about what's going on?" She calmly replied, "No, because I knew that you were going to call back today and would tell me what to do next." "Wow" was the only thought that came to mind in that moment. This parent was counting on my follow-up phone call to inform the school.

As the year continued for Melvin, he eventually had the transplant, went through a season of recuperation, and graduated on time with his class.

Homework

1. How is your reputation diminished because of not following through on your words?

_____

_____

_____

_____

_____

2. Give an example of a person that you deem as trustworthy because of their follow through?

_____

_____

_____

_____

_____

_____

Extended Lesson – Create your motto/quotation that will govern your commitment to follow through.

_____

_____

_____

_____

_____

_____

_____

_____

_____

Reminders –

1. Follow-through is if I say that I am going to do something I will do it.

2. It is in follow-through that trust is built or trust is destroyed. A lack of follow-though is viewed by students as empty promises.

Unit 3 – What Happens When You Care?

The Law of Cause and Effect, as outlined by Sir Isaac Newton, says that "For every action there is an equal and opposite reaction." Other researchers view this law as the principle of sow and reap—"you reap what you sow." This law has an impact on everyday living.

As we continue to examine the tenets of care, it is necessary to determine the effects of care. If you . . .

1. Feel interest in your students

2. Are concerned about your students

3. Have a liking, fondness for your students

4. Provide help, protection, or supervision to your students

5. Look after and provide for the needs of your students

6. Are devoted to; to think the world of your students

They will be affected! They will listen to you, they will care as a result, and they will follow your example.

This will be their response because they will *see* that you are relatable—a real person with real issues and real approaches to addressing those issues.

This will also be their response because they will *see* that you are passionately speaking with conviction to them as though their life was your own, yet patiently listening without distraction and judgment to them.

NOTE: It's not what you say, rather the motivation behind how you say it that portrays care.

Question – What motivates you to work with young people?

Care won't happen if the motivation is missing or is incorrect or has been weakened by situations and circumstances seen, experienced, or perceived by the adult.

It is up to YOU to regain your motivation. You must remain mindful of "why" you are working with our young people. Our actions will cause a reaction. Hopefully it will be one where the student is better because you cared.

"Care is a two-way street. You must listen to the person to really hear their concern or just what they have to say, and then act accordingly to what they actually need. Sometimes, to care, you don't need to say or do anything—you just need to listen and maybe even give a hug. Care is giving someone what they need, not what they want. It is helping them to see something they didn't know they needed. Care is support. It has to be true and genuine."

—Ebony McSwain, class of 2008

Lesson 1 –
Your Voice Matters

"What do YOU think?"

Everyday people make over a thousand decisions—what to wear, what to eat, who to call, text or email!! Not every decision is that simple though. In those instances, it is necessary to seek counsel for their input or guidance in making a good decision.

Sometimes for our students, they seek our counsel. **Please be warned**—not every adult will be considered to help them in making their decisions. They are looking for the person(s) who have shown them care. Those who know them, those who listen to them without distraction and without judgment, and those who speak to them with passion and conviction about them.

When you speak, can they feel that you care? Do they sense that you are speaking to them as though they are a son or a daughter, a little sister or little brother? Are you speaking as though "YOUR life depends on it!"?

When you care, your opinion will matter to your students. They will seek you—via a phone call, a text message, an email, or a face-to-face conversation. When we encounter these scenarios, it's imperative that we are mindful of what we say or don't say and how we respond.

Sidelinger et. al (2016) cites Tinto's interactionalist theory, which asserts that effective classroom interactions enhance student learning and persistence. He hypothesizes that "students who meaningfully interact with instructors demonstrate greater educational development and learning gains; thus when students are involved with faculty they succeed." Additionally, "students who experience rapport with their instructors may feel comfortable interacting with them outside of class and may seek that instructor to help with academic-related issues" (p. 168).

Bonnie's Story

For about four years, I taught Life Skills. In this class, we discussed a myriad of topics from short-term goals and financial planning to gearing up for your freshman year in college. Periodically, I would share personal stories with my students to aid them in making their decisions.

After graduating from high school, Bonnie decided to attend college out of state and to major in computer engineering. We were excited for Bonnie because she had been accepted into a prestigious university with a reputable engineering program.

On Bonnie's first visit back home, she and I briefly discussed her adjustment to college life and her roommate. She answered my questions. On her next visit, the conversation was similar. Prior to her spring break, she texted me, "I need to see you when I come home next week." I simply replied, "OK."

Bonnie came to my classroom at the end of the school day and sat at a desk in a slouched position. "What's up?" I asked. "I want to change my major and come closer to home, but I don't know how to tell my dad." Calmly I said, "OK. What do you want to change your major to?" She answered. I could relate to her because I had a similar experience in college, so I shared it with her and attempted to provide her with reassurance that her dad would understand.

A few days later, she texted me, "I told him, and he is OK! Thanks!" My only response was a smile. Bonnie changed schools at the end of the school year and began to soar. Today she is working in her new field and soon will be the owner of her company. Both of her parents are proud supporters of her endeavors.

Homework

1. Do you speak to your students as though "YOUR" life depends on it? Why or why not? Explain your response.

_____

_____

_____

_____

_____

_____

_____

_____

_____

_____

_____

_____

_____

2. Reflect on a time when you knew that a person desired your opinion before making a decision. How did you approach the conversation?

_____

_____

_____

_____

_____

_____

_____

_____

_____

_____

_____

_____

"Care looks like the compassion you have for someone—a selfless act that won't benefit you. It is the ability to give of yourself to someone who doesn't know you."

Jerome Miller, Jr., class of 2009

Lesson 2 –
You Replicate Care

"She cared for me, so I'll care for you"

I like the cliché, "Monkey see; monkey do!" Oftentimes we become a carbon copy of what we see. Sometimes what we see yields good results; other times not so good results. **Please note:** When one experiences care, he or she will replicate it.

Replicate means to repeat or to be the same as another. Because care is an act of the heart, it touches the heart of the recipient; and the recipient is changed. Their outlook may be changed, their opinion or perspective may be changed, and their life may be forever changed. This is the great impact of care. Once your life is impacted, you are now compelled to do the same for someone else.

Care is contagious; it is truly passed from one person to another person.

Bruce Bacon's Story

Throughout my middle and high school years, I had really good teachers. They showed me care, constantly reminded me of my purpose, and encouraged me to be my best.

When I returned to my alma mater to teach shortly after graduating from college, I was presented with my first opportunity to teach the son of one of my former teachers—Bruce Y. Bacon. He was an animated, fun-loving student. He was also hard-working, opinionated, and at times, stubborn.

Still a novice teacher, I took great pride in having rules and high expectations for my classes. I was known for having a serious demeanor and for being consistent; however, things would change when Bruce Bacon entered the classroom. He knew how to make the class (and me) laugh. At times, he would resemble the type of student that I was in high school; but I was reminded of how patient his mom was with me. I felt a sense of indebtedness to Bruce Bacon because of the care that his mom had shown me.

For the remainder of his high school years, Bruce Bacon remained in close communication with me; and I simply provided a listening ear for him. Like the care that his mom provided me in college, Bruce and I communicated throughout his years in college. I would never miss a birthday, and he would always tell me about honor society inductions, scholarship opportunities, and summer internships.

Bruce Bacon had one promise to me that, I believe, is connected to replicated care. He told me "that his first one million dollars would be given to me for my kids!" Although Bruce Bacon is not an educator, he still desires to replicate care by giving back to those that cared for him. I'm counting on Bruce (and so many others)!

Homework

1. What are some things that you do or phrases that you say because of someone who cared for you?

_____

_____

_____

_____

_____

_____

_____

_____

_____

_____

2. What are some of your attributes that are worth following?

_____

_____

_____

_____

_____

_____

_____

_____

_____

_____

_____

Extended Lesson – Write a letter, email, or post to the teacher, school leader, coach, or mentor that impacted your decision to care for others.

"Care is taking the time to nurture/ provide for those you're responsible and concerned for."

Brianna Peppins, class of 2013

Lesson 3 –
You're Worth Following

"I see myself in you!"

One of the coolest aspects of school is that students are typically in school for approximately 13–17 years. Over that span of time, they encounter over 100 teachers, aides, librarians, coaches, secretaries, bus drivers, school leaders, security, and more. Sometimes they will encounter staff that resemble their life—their demeanor, their attitude, their outlook and perspective, or their background. It causes the staff member to seem more relatable, and the child will feel more comfortable and willing to establish a relationship with them.

There are some children, however, that will not voice their admiration with a staff member but will strive to imitate or replicate what they see. As the educators, we must be mindful that our students are watching us; and some of them are looking to you to know what path to follow in life.

Maddy's Story

As I have shared before, I started teaching when I was in the 10th grade. I was an afterschool dance teacher for children in grades 1st – 8th grade. Maddy and I met when she was in the 1st grade. She regularly attended class and worked hard. It was her hard work and energy that consistently permitted her to dance on the first row (which is an honor in the dance world).

Later, she became one of my students at my alma mater. She was still a hard worker and still danced. By this time, she was deemed one of the school leaders, well trusted by the staff and respected by her peers. Most of our conversations were around her need to remain focused on being successful.

While she was in college, we stayed connected. Near the end of her college years, she returned home to work with me and others in summer youth programming. Over the next few summers, she learned how to do "my" job in facilitating activities.

Once she graduated from college, she expressed her willingness to return to our alma mater to teach. I was ecstatic!! She got the job, and I had a few years to coach her as a new teacher.

Today we are still working on the same staff, where I am now watching her make connections with her students. I overhear conversations among the students about Maddy and how they love her.

Recently she gave me a gift that read, "friend, forever, irreplaceable." This gift was quite meaningful to me because I realized that my life has served as a blueprint to aid Maddy in her navigation for success.

Homework

1. How would you respond if one of your students referred to you as "friend, forever, irreplaceable"?

_____

_____

_____

_____

_____

_____

_____

_____

_____

_____

2. Are you worth following? Explain your response.

_____

_____

_____

_____

_____

_____

_____

_____

_____

_____

_____

_____

_____

_____

_____

_____

Extended Lesson – List all of the people who influenced you to be the person that you are. Contact them to say, "Thank You."

_____

_____

_____

_____

_____

_____

_____

_____

_____

_____

_____

_____

_____

_____

Unit 4 – Care Anyway

As we prepare to conclude this book, let's review the definitions of care.

1. To feel interest in something

2. To be concerned about

3. To have a liking, fondness

4. To provide help, protection, or supervision to

5. To look after and provide for the needs of

6. To be devoted to; to think the world of

In reading this book, you have been challenged to examine your motivation for working with today's children. You have reflected on the people who influenced your decision to work with today's children. You have also been reminded of the long-term impact that YOU can have on our future leaders.

There is one more word that we must consider to keep us in place to be loving and effective teachers, coaches, school leaders, mentors, and more. That word is "distract." Distract is defined as

1. To draw the mind to a different object

2. To stir up or confuse with conflicting emotions or motives

3. To divert (to turn from a course or purpose)

As educators, we cannot allow ourselves to be distracted by what we see, what we encounter, what we experience, or what we perceive. As our students are confronted even earlier with the ills of society, they have an even greater need for caring teachers.

Research shows that within the first five years for a novice teacher, 20% to 50% of them will leave the profession. Some may propose that online education is a suitable replacement for the missing teachers. Computers can provide instruction; however, only a teacher can look into a child's eye to reassure him or her that they are smart. Only a teacher can dry the eyes of a child who is saddened by the death of a loved one. Only a teacher can have a hidden drawer with snacks for students that are hungry and wondering from where the next meal will come.

Educators, we can't get distracted. We can't feel defeated. We can't quit caring for our students. We must stick to it and care anyway!

"Care is a reflection of love. When you love, you care; and if you care about someone or something, it generally means there is some love there . . . Sometimes care came in a way that I didn't appreciate at first but became grateful for when I realized its meaning. Like when my mom would tell me that I needed to fix my attitude and learn to count my blessings, or when my advisor would tell me that if I didn't fix my attitude towards school I'd never get my GPA together. It's those moments in life that remind us that if it were not for someone who cared for us we would not be who we are today.

Care is also a reflection of our heart condition towards others. It is because someone cared for me, that I can now care for others. Just like God cared for us that He gave us Jesus, so can we care for others."

Jahari Mercer, class of 2015

Lesson 1 –
Love Never Fails. . .

"Regardless of how you act!"

The Bible teaches that "love never fails." This verse is embodied in our teachers, coaches, school leaders, mentors, and more. The words prior to this verse are also worth considering.

> "Love endures with patience and serenity, love is kind and thoughtful . . . love does not brag and is not proud or arrogant. It is not rude; it is not self-seeking, it is not provoked [nor overly sensitive and easily angered]; it does not take into account a wrong endured. Love bears all things [regardless of what comes], believes all things [looking for the best in each one], hopes all things [remaining steadfast during difficult times], endures all things [without weakening]."
>
> —I Corinthians 13:4–5, 7 (AMP)

Although the instructions may seem daunting, the commitment to love and to care for our students—regardless—will prove beneficial.

As caring educators, we must

1. Be patient and calm with our students.

2. Be kind and mindful of our responses (verbal and non-verbal) to our students.

3. Be humble and willing to apologize when wrong to our students.

4. Look for the good in EVERY student. (It's easy to find the bad in a situation; be DIFFERENT! Find the good and stand out with your students.)

5. Not be rude towards our students. (Remember that you are the adult working with children.)

6. Not be overly sensitive and easily angered by our students. (Please don't take mistreatment personally.)

7. Remain, even when students or your environment become difficult.

I am not proposing that caring educators must be held captive to mistreatment; however, I am strongly asking you to reconsider your attitude the next time you have a less than pleasant encounter with a student.

All it takes is for you to have a change of mind for your students. Over time, they will notice it, acknowledge it, and acquiesce to your desired behavior and expectations. When you love, it shows!

Story of the Class of 2013

In my third year as a teacher at my alma mater, I found myself with the class of 2013 for two periods. I was their English teacher and their Bible teacher. I liked this class, but it was quite evident that they did not like each other. Their disdain for one another sometimes made the classroom controversial and adversarial. In speaking with the students and my principal, I was willing to adjust my classroom so that most of our time was spent on teaching and learning.

Because I knew that I was not going to quit on these students or ignore their poor treatment towards each other, I was reminded that "love never fails." For about a week, this class was responsible for creating a LOVE mural to be one of the bulletin boards in the classroom. The caveat was that they were assigned to groups with individuals of whom they did not get along.

Oh, boy! The first two days were noisy, but I was resolute in not changing the groups or the assignment. Some groups chose to work after school because they realized that they had not made good use of class time. Once the project was completed and they assembled the board, they were proud. They were proud of their group members and proud of the class. I was proud of them because they taught me that love is patient and endures for a long time.

In the years to come, they continued to work on loving each other. At times, they would reminisce on their LOVE mural project and how immature they were. By graduation night, they charged the underclassmen to love each other and to be kind. They stressed the importance of forgiving others for childhood hurts. They concluded the night by affectionately referring to themselves as the LOVE Bunch!

Homework

1. Which element of LOVE is your strength?

_____

_____

_____

_____

_____

_____

_____

_____

_____

_____

_____

_____

2. Which element of LOVE is your weakness and the one for which you will commit to improve?

_____

_____

_____

_____

Extended Lesson – If you were to resign from your current position, what impact would it have on your students?

_____

_____

_____

_____

_____

_____

_____

"Care, to me, means you put aside your personal life to pour into the lives of others. Care means we share life experiences and grow together. If I'm going through a difficult time, you find a way to help me see I can be successful no matter the challenge."

Jasmine Grandison, class of 2009

Lesson 2 – A Calm Answer Changes Things

"Regardless of what you say"

In this era of social media and Internet-usage, children and adults use them as platforms to be heard. Years ago, I concluded that there are very few people who desire to listen to others because everyone wants to be heard.

Some students come from large families and don't feel heard. Some have experienced countless times of disappointment, rejection, and a lack of adult follow-through. This feeling manifests itself in constant inquiry, reluctance, and hesitance to trust adults. Others are in classrooms where they feel ignored and therefore must create ways to be seen and to be heard.

This phenomenon often presents itself in loud, aggressive speech and overly expressive behaviors. As the educators, we cannot allow ourselves to get distracted by a child's indirect cry for love, care, and attention. We must give it to them—calmly. Calmly—because this aggressive behavior is often reciprocated by the educator (that I assume is caught off guard).

Proverbs 15:1 provides us with a blueprint for our responses. "A soft and gentle and thoughtful answer turns away wrath [anger, displeasure, rage]. But harsh and painful and careless words stir up anger."

Based on our personality and rapport with our students, it is imperative that our responses don't harm them. Regardless of what is said to us, as educators, our response must be thoughtful, nurturing, and caring. It should still reassure the student that you are fond of him or her regardless of what is being said or done.

Story of the Class of 2017

As I started at a new school, I learned early that I was working in a loud building. Adults and students needed to be heard. Although vigilant, I decided to take a different approach to reaching students. Remain calm no matter what.

Every morning, I sat at my duty post, calmly greeted every person—staff and students—"Good morning!" and answered students' questions. Although the building was loud, my space remained calm.

As the year continued, I would be confronted with loud, inquisitive students that needed answers immediately. Without raising my voice, I calmly replied, "Give me one second because I want to make sure that you are getting my undivided attention." Quite shocked by my answer, the students would wait, calm down, and be able to share their concern or to make their request without yelling.

Overtime, the word spread that I would "take care of you" if you just talk to me. After graduation, two young men, Morris and Nelson, stopped by to see me. As the conversation was concluding, they commented that it was evident that I cared for them regardless of what they said or what they did. They jokingly said, "I don't know how you stayed so calm with us because we know that we were a handful!" I laughed with them but realized that this approach had worked!

Homework

1. What could prevent you from responding to situations calmly?

---

2. What are the long-term effects of harsh, painful, and careless words?

_____

_____

_____

_____

_____

_____

_____

Extended Lesson – Rehearse your responses to the following scenarios with a colleague.

1. Student steals your phone and returns to class after being suspended.

2. You have reminded a student about a school rule, but the student does not comply.

3. Student-athlete is failing classes due to attendance.

"Caring is setting aside your personal needs or wants to contribute to another's happiness. It can also be defined as fully giving someone or something your undivided time and placing forth your best effort."

—Quentin McSwain, class of 2010

Lesson 3 – Get Some (parental) Help

"Parents are KEY!"

At the start of the school year, teachers have a plethora of tasks to address—set up the classroom, attend workshops, review rosters, IEPs, and 504 plans, prepare lesson plans, and so much more. Teachers are also encouraged to contact the students' parents by the end of the first month to introduce themselves and to foster a relationship with the parents.

As a former assistant principal, this was the area of most resistance. The push back was always around not having enough time to do everything else and to call parents. I would suggest that we make time for what is important.

As it pertains to educating our students, their parents are the key to our success. We can't forget that they birthed them, are raising them, and know their child's strengths and weaknesses. We have a limited amount of time to get to know them, and their parents' input is vital. Additionally, a parent's voice, for most students, ignites a level of fear that gets their attention and causes things to change.

As educators, we must welcome the parents to our classrooms. We must welcome the parents to the learning process. We must welcome the parents to the educational team for their child, for parents are key.

Quincy's Story

One school year, it was decided that all Student Government Association (SGA) officers would be staff-appointed and accepted by the students. As we interviewed the students, most of them were elated that they had been selected and were looking forward to working.

Quincy was the exception.

Quincy was an intelligent, hard-working young man that was well-mannered and respectful. Quincy also played two sports—football and baseball. When Quincy entered the interview, he seemed quite casual and slightly dismissive. As we began to share how his attributes mirrored that of a leader and the role we desired for him to play, he simply replied, "I'm not a leader; I'm an athlete." We worked a little bit more to convince him that he could lead in his sport and transfer the skill to school. Politely yet directly, Quincy said, "Thanks for this opportunity, but I'm not interested." We thanked him for attending the interview and adjourned the meeting.

The SGA advisor gave our principal an update on the interviews and shared the results of Quincy's interview. The principal immediately recants, "I'm calling his dad." You see, the principal had a rapport with his dad and knew what he desired for his children. He realized that this dad needed to be informed of his son's outlook.

In the conversation with Quincy's dad, he thanked the principal for calling. He also admitted that he was guilty of placing more attention on developing Quincy as an athlete instead of being a leader. He noted, "this will change." He asked if he could have a training role for this year to expose his son to new possibilities. Our principal thought that Quincy's dad's recommendation was good and agreed to it.

That year, Quincy was not installed into SGA; however, he trained under some of the other leaders. He attended meetings, helped plan events, and garnered support from his peers. The next school year, Quincy was interviewed for SGA and gladly accepted the role. He remained in SGA for three out of his four years of high school. By his senior year, he was grooming other leaders, especially male athletes, to take his role in the future. Although he was an athlete, he enthusiastically made time for SGA; not because his dad made him but because he shared with him the importance of being a leader.

Near the end of his senior year, Quincy and I would laugh about his initial response to SGA. I would challenge him by saying that one day he may own a sports' team instead of playing for one. Quincy has since graduated from high school and college with a bachelor's and master's degree.

He has even worked in the marketing department for a local professional sports team. Who knows? Quincy might have still been aspiring to play for these teams instead of completing his education if his dad had not been called.

Homework

1. What reservation do you have in communicating with parents?

_____

_____

_____

_____

_____

_____

_____

_____

_____

_____

_____

2. How would you respond to a disgruntle parent?

_____

_____

_____

_____

_____

_____

_____

Extended Lesson – Contact the parents of a student who is giving you the most trouble and use the sandwich approach of support.

1. State something positive about the child.

2. Identify and discuss 1–2 areas of concern to be strengthened or improved.

3. Close with reassurance that you are committed to the child's overall success.

4. Ask the parent for questions.

"Care looks like taking care of those who need it without looking for anything in return. Care looks like a mother holding her newborn baby. Care looks like a father carrying his baby girl on his shoulders at the county fair. Care looks like love transferred from one person to another.

—Angelina Taylor, class of 2016

Closing – Why Am I Here?

There will be a class that causes you to ask, "Why am I here? Why do I continue to be an educator when there are other professional pursuits for which I aspire to attain? Why do I care when it seems like it doesn't matter??

These are not questions that I can answer because I never could find the answer. In that class (fill in the blank), all I saw were young, innocent, and sincere faces looking back at me, expecting me to stick by their sides. All I experienced were our future leaders, seeking approval, validation, and celebration. All I remember is the one child's mom who said, "this was my son's first time 'getting it!' Thanks!"

We care because it makes a difference.

We care because it changes lives forever.

We care because we must care.

Our students are counting on us!

REFERENCES

Larson, R. W., & Verma, S. (1999). How children and adolescents spend time across the world: Work, play, and developmental opportunities. *Psychological Bulletin*, *125*(6), 701-736. doi:10.1037/0033-2909.125.6.701

Sidelinger, R. J., Frisby, B. N., & Heisler, J. (2016). Students' out of the classroom communication with instructors and campus services: Exploring social integration and academic involvement. *Learning and Individual Differences*, *47*167-171. doi:10.1016/j.lindif.2016.02.011

Yssel, N., Engelbrecht, P., Oswald, M., Eloff, I., & Swart, E. (2007). Views of inclusion: a comparative study of parents' perceptions in South Africa and the United States. *Remedial & Special Education*, *28*(6), 356-365. doi:10.1177/07419325070280060501

ABOUT THE AUTHOR

 Tisa M. Holley has been an educator in K – 12 settings for 15 years. She has worked in public, private, and charter schools. As a teacher, school counselor, basketball and cheer coach, SGA advisor, and assistant principal, she has always worked in the best interest of children.

Now, as an author, she seeks to transfer her knowledge, skills, and passion to others that work with children. She believes that every encounter with a teacher, coach, mentor, or school leader, whether positive or negative, will influence our future adults. Therefore, it is imperative that each encounter is meaningful and impactful.

Tisa is a proud alumna of Florida A&M University and Regent University and resides in Maryland. In her spare time, she is a motivational speaker for children and teens.

To schedule a speaking engagement, visit www.themissingpart.org.

SELF-PUBLISHING
SCHOOL

NOW IT'S YOUR TURN

Discover the EXACT 3-step blueprint you need to become a bestselling author in 3 months.

Self-Publishing School helped me, and now I want them to help you with this FREE WEBINAR!

Even if you're busy, bad at writing, or don't know where to start, you CAN write a bestseller and build your best life.

With tools and experience across a variety of niches and professions, Self-Publishing School is the only resource you need to take your book to the finish line!

DON'T WAIT

Watch this FREE WEBINAR now, and Say "YES" to becoming a bestseller:

https://xe172.isrefer.com/go/sps4fta-vts/YoungTim

Made in USA - North Chelmsford, MA
1024121_9780692083772
11 15 2019 1632